DINOSAUR WORLD

# Monster Fish
## The Adventure of the Ichthyosaurs

Written by Michael Dahl

Illustrated by Garry Nichols

Special thanks to our advisers for their expertise:

Content Adviser: Philip J. Currie, Curator of Dinosaurs, Royal Tyrrell Museum of Palaeontology, Drumheller, Alberta, Canada

Reading Adviser: Susan Kesselring, M.A., Literacy Educator, Rosemount - Apple Valley - Eagan (Minnesota) School District

PICTURE WINDOW BOOKS
Minneapolis, Minnesota

Managing Editor: Catherine Neitge
Creative Director: Terri Foley
Art Director: Keith Griffin
Editor: Patricia Stockland
Designer: Joe Anderson
Page production: Picture Window Books
The illustrations in this book were prepared digitally.

Picture Window Books
5115 Excelsior Boulevard
Suite 232
Minneapolis, MN 55416
877-845-8392
www.picturewindowbooks.com

Printed in the United States of America.

**Library of Congress Cataloging-in-Publication Data**
Dahl, Michael.
Monster fish : the adventure of the Ichthyosaurs / written by
Michael Dahl ; illustrated by Garry Nichols.
p. cm. — (Dinosaur world)
Includes bibliographical references and index.
ISBN 1-4048-0941-4 (hardcover)
ISBN 1-4048-1836-7 (paperback)
1. Ichthyosaurus—Pictorial works—Juvenile literature.
I. Nichols, Garry, 1958- ill. II. Title.

QE862.I2D33 2004
567.9'37—dc22                    2004019921

No humans lived during the time of the dinosaurs. No person heard them roar, saw their scales, or felt their feathers.

The giant creatures are gone, but their fossils, or remains, lie hidden in the earth. Dinosaur skulls, skeletons, and eggs have been buried in rock for millions of years.

All around the world, scientists dig up fossils and carefully study them. Bones show how tall the dinosaurs stood. Claws and teeth show how they grabbed and what they ate. Scientists compare fossils with the bodies of living creatures such as birds and reptiles, which are relatives of the dinosaurs. Every year, scientists learn more and more about the giants that have disappeared.

Studying fossils and figuring out how the dinosaurs lived is like putting together the pieces of a puzzle that is millions of years old.

This is what some of those pieces can tell us about the swimming creatures known as ichthyosaurs (IK-thee-oh-sors).

Hundreds of millions of years ago, a giant ocean stretched halfway around the world. Its warm waves covered shallow seabeds and deep trenches. In this ocean swam many creatures known as ichthyosaurs.

Sunlight sparkled on the back of a giant swimmer. The swimmer curved above the waves, filled its lungs with a breath of air, then vanished with a giant splash. Along the ocean surface swam the creature called *Ophthalmosaurus* (off-THOL-mo-sore-us), one type of ichthyosaur.

*Ophthalmosaurus* was not a dinosaur. It was a sea reptile that lived during the Age of the Dinosaurs. *Ophthalmosaurus* was a type of creature known as an ichthyosaur, which means "fish lizard." Many different types of ichthyosaurs swam and hunted in the world's first oceans.

*Ophthalmosaurus* plunged into the water. Its four strong fins pushed the creature deep into the shadows. A crescent tail helped turn its long, sleek body while hunting for food.

A trail of bubbles rose from its nostrils.
*Ophthalmosaurus* dove straight downward.

Ichthyosaurs looked like dolphins. They had long,
smooth bodies, pointed snouts, and curved fins.
Ichthyosaurs spent all of their time in the ocean, but
they needed to come to the surface for air.

Dim sunlight reached down into the water. As *Ophthalmosaurus* swam through a deep trench, the pupils widened in its enormous eyes. The swimmer stared left and right, searching for food in the shifting shadows.

Ophthalmosaurus means "eye lizard." Fossils of the creature show eye sockets that are over 4 inches wide (23 centimeters). Its eyeballs were the size of coconuts. They could adjust quickly to the dark, like a cat's eyes.

9

*Ophthalmosaurus* glided around a curve of the canyon and found its prey. Darting ahead was a school of squiggling, squid-like belemnites.

*Ophthalmosaurus*, like all other ichthyosaurs, was a predator. It hunted other creatures for food. The fish-lizard had strong, sharp teeth and a diet that included shelled creatures called ammonites, as well as small fish, crabs, eels, and ocean insects.

*Ophthalmosaurus* opened its long, pointed snout. A flip of its strong fins shot the hunter toward the squid creatures.

A vast shadow appeared above the ichthyosaur. The shadow blotted out the sunlight. Enormous jaws spread wide, and the belemnites vanished.

The shadow swung around, sending ripples through the water. *Ophthalmosaurus* blinked its giant eyes. Ahead loomed the sea monster *Temnodontosaurus*.

*Temnodontosaurus* ("cutting tooth lizard") was a large, powerful ichthyosaur. Its torpedo-shaped body could grow up to 30 feet (9 meters) long, three times the size of a normal *Ophthalmosaurus*. *Ophthalmosaurus* could grow up to twice the size of an adult human.

*Temnodontosaurus* gobbled the last of the squid creatures. Its long jaws crunched the sharp hooks on the belemnite's wiggling arms. The belemnite squirted ink to try to hide itself from *Temnodontosaurus*, but it was too late.

The stomach contents of many ichthyosaur fossils show the remains of squid-creatures, like belemnites. Scientists think that prehistoric squids were a favorite meal of *Ophthalmosaurus*.

*Ophthalmosaurus* watched and waited, looking for any remaining scraps. But with an ocean full of fish and other creatures, *Ophthalmosaurus* could easily find more food.

Slowly, the larger reptile turned and started swimming away. Two more *Ophthalmosaurses* raced into view. They were not hunting. They were fleeing.

A silent shadow, more colossal than *Temnodontosaurus,* suddenly surged into view. *Liopleurodon* (lie-oh-PLOOR-uh-don) was the largest carnivore on Earth. Its fearsome, needle-sharp teeth grabbed an ichthyosaur and shook it from side to side.

*Liopleurodon* was not a dinosaur or an ichthyosaur. It was half-shark, half-crocodile, with a head twice the size of a *T. rex*'s head. *Liopleurodon*'s streamlined body stretched 75 feet (25 meters) long. That's as long as two school buses.

*Ophthalmosaurus* fled through the ocean canyon. *Liopleurodon* raced after it.

*Ophthalmosaurus* could swim quickly, but it did not have the power of modern-day dolphins. The ichthyosaur was only good at racing in short bursts and could not keep up a fast pace for very long. But because of its vast size, *Liopleurodon* could not move as quickly as the big-eyed ichthyosaur.

*Ophthalomosaurus* spied a narrow canyon. With a mighty twitch of hind muscles, it swiftly turned and rushed toward safety. *Liopleurodon* opened its gigantic jaws and sped toward the frightened swimmer.

*Liopleurodon* stopped. It could not enter the narrow, rocky opening that *Ophthalmosaurus* had entered.

With a rush of bubbles, *Liopleurodon* swam away from the canyon and vanished from view.

*Ophthalomosaurus* hovered in the shadows of the canyon's close walls. Soon it would need to surface for air, but for now, all was safe.

## Ichthyosaurs: Where ...

Ichthyosaur fossils have been discovered on nearly every continent. They have been found in South America, Central America, Canada, Greenland, Japan, Germany, and England as well as in the United States. The ichthyosaur is the state fossil of Nevada.

## ... and When

The "Age of Dinosaurs" began 248 million years ago (mya). If we imagine the time from the beginning of the dinosaur age to the present as one day, the Age of Dinosaurs lasted 18 hours—and humans have only been around for 10 minutes!

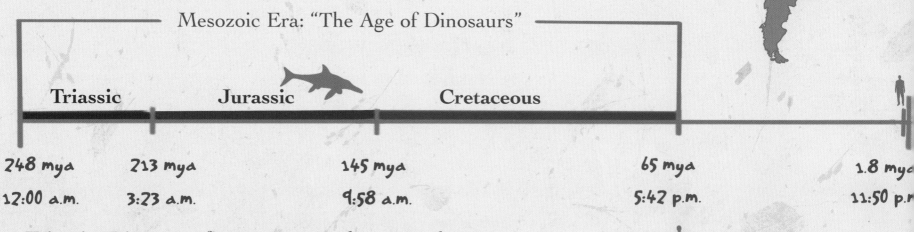

Mesozoic Era: "The Age of Dinosaurs"

| Triassic | Jurassic | Cretaceous | | |
|---|---|---|---|---|
| 248 mya | 213 mya | 145 mya | 65 mya | 1.8 mya |
| 12:00 a.m. | 3:23 a.m. | 9:58 a.m. | 5:42 p.m. | 11:50 p.m. |

**Triassic**—Dinosaurs first appear. Early mammals appear.
**Jurassic**—First birds appear.
**Cretaceous**—Flowering plants appear. By the end of this era, all dinosaurs disappear.

—When humans arrived

—Ichthyosaurs lived

# Digging Deeper

## One Ocean

Scientists believe that millions of years ago, all the world's continents were squeezed into one "super-continent" called Pangea. This left the rest of the earth covered by a single ocean. Some scientists call it the Tethys (TETH-iss) Ocean. Tethys was the name of an ancient Greek goddess of the sea. Ichthyosaurs probably traveled throughout the entire ocean, which was the same temperature everywhere on Earth.

## Spewing Shells

Ichthyosaur vomit has been discovered in a rock quarry in England. Scientists who examined the prehistoric lunch found it full of bits of belemnite shells. Ichthyosaurs probably regurgitated the shells after chewing the belemnites, just as whales spew squid shells. By throwing up the hard body parts of their dinner, the ichthyosaurs would not damage the soft tissues of their own digestive systems.

## Eye Bones

Ichthyosaurs had special bones inside their giant eyes. The bones called "sclerotic rings" looked like donuts. When ichthyosaurs dived deep into the ocean, powerful water pressure pushed against their eyes. The bony rings kept the eyes round, unharmed, and working clearly.

## Last Meal

No one knows why the ichthyosaurs vanished from the world's waterways. Scientists have discovered that at the same time the fish-lizards disappeared, other stronger, shark-like creatures were beginning to hunt the seas. Perhaps the ichthyosaurs all ended up as dinner. More likely, the shark creatures were stronger predators that ate all the ichthyosaurs' food.

## Words to Know

**carnivore**—a creature that eats only meat, or other living creatures

**dinosaurs**—giant creatures that lived millions of years ago; scientists think that many modern reptiles and birds are related to dinosaurs

**predator**—an animal that hunts other animals for food

**prey**—the animal hunted by a predator

**reptile**—animals covered in scaly skin, like lizards, crocodiles, or turtles; many reptiles live in the water

**squid**—sea animal with a long, tube-shaped body and ten wavy arms; some squid have shells

# To Learn More

## At the Library

Barlowe, Wayne, and Peter Dodson. *An Alphabet of Dinosaurs.*
  New York: Scholastic, 1995.

Cohen, Daniel. *Ichthyosaurs.* Mankato, Minn.: Bridgestone Books, 2003.

Rodriguez, K.S. *Ichthyosaurus.* Austin, Tex.: Steadwell Books, 2000.

## On the Web

FactHound offers a safe, fun way to find Web sites related to this book. All of the sites on FactHound have been researched by our staff. *www.facthound.com*

1. Visit the FactHound home page.
2. Enter a search word related to this book,
   or type in this special code: 1404809414
3. Click on the FETCH IT button.

Your trusty FactHound will fetch the best Web sites for you!